WEALTH BUILDING
THE SECRET TO BUILDING GENERATIONAL WEALTH WITH REAL ESTATE

BY

JOHNSON RYAN

TABLE OF CONTENTS

CHAPTER 1: INTRODUCTION

Welcome to "Wealth Building: The Secret to Building Generational Wealth with Real Estate." In this introduction, we will set out on a journey to discover the hidden gems of financial wealth and the enormous impact real estate can have on leaving lasting legacies.

As we delve into the fundamentals of wealth creation, we'll look at the necessity of laying solid financial foundations, comprehending the distinct benefits of real estate investments, and developing long-term strategy. This guide is your compass, guiding you through the complex landscape of financial success and delivering insights that go beyond individual benefits, with the goal of creating generational wealth.

Prepare to discover the mysteries, face the obstacles, and seize the possibilities that await you. This is only the beginning of a journey into the transforming potential of deliberate wealth creation. The pages that follow will equip you to leave a legacy that will last for centuries. In this introduction, we lay the stage for a deep dive into the world of wealth creation, concentrating on the often-overlooked treasure trove of generational wealth through real estate. Our journey begins by emphasizing the crucial need of building the foundations for long-term prosperity by having a solid financial foundation.

We'll examine the riddles of real estate investments' unique ability to shape not only personal wealth but also long-lasting legacies that echo through time. By following the ideas provided in this guide, you will acquire insights into developing tactics that will withstand the test of time.

Importance of Building Generational Wealth

Building generational wealth is critical because it extends beyond individual financial achievement, leaving a lasting influence that spans numerous generations. Here are some main reasons for the significance:

Legacy and Security: Generational wealth provides a financial safety net for future family members, providing financial security that can weather economic changes. It becomes a legacy that may be passed down to future generations, providing stability and assurance.

Educational possibilities: Future generations can benefit from accumulated money in order to obtain greater educational possibilities. This, in turn, gives people the confidence to pursue their goals, encouraging a circle of continual progress and knowledge transfer.

Entrepreneurial Ventures: Generational wealth offers the resources required to support family entrepreneurial efforts. This can result in the establishment of new firms, innovations, and job opportunities, all of which contribute to economic growth and sustainability.

Homeownership and Real Estate: Real estate investments are frequently used to build wealth over generations. Property ownership becomes a physical asset that not only grows in value over time but also acts as a residence and a source of generational wealth through inheritance.

Financial Freedom and Options: Building money provides future generations with more financial freedom and options. They can pursue occupations out of enthusiasm rather than necessity, participate in philanthropy, and positively impact their communities.

Social Impact: Family wealth enables them to participate in philanthropy and social causes. Families with the financial wherewithal to give to charity causes can have a long-term impact on society, leaving a beneficial legacy for future generations.

Cultural and Personal Values: In addition to passing down riches, cultural and personal values can be passed down. Families may develop a feeling of responsibility, financial discipline, and ethical considerations in their children, benefiting both the family and the community as a whole.

In essence, the significance of generational wealth is based on its potential to leave a lasting legacy, provide opportunities for future generations, and positively contribute to society, so fostering a circle of prosperity and success.

Overview of Wealth Building Principles

A collection of fundamental ideas that constitute the core of financial success drive the wealth-building path. Here's a rundown of these critical wealth-creation principles:

Financial Education: Understanding the fundamentals of personal money, investing, and economic trends gives the groundwork for making informed decisions. Individuals can traverse the complexity of wealth building with the help of continuous learning.

Setting clear short-term and long-term financial goals provides direction and incentive. Goals act as benchmarks, allowing individuals to track their progress and make strategic decisions that are in line with their aims.

Budgeting and Saving: Creating and sticking to a realistic budget provides for better management of income and expenses. Even little amounts saved on a regular basis contribute to the growth of wealth over time.

Debt Management: It is critical for financial health to manage and reduce debt wisely. Prioritizing high-interest debt and adhering to a strict repayment schedule frees up resources for wealth-building activities.

Diversification of assets: Spreading investments across different asset classes reduces risk and improves overall portfolio stability. Stocks, bonds, real estate, and other investment vehicles can all be included in diversification.

Compound Interest: Using compound interest to increase investments allows them to expand exponentially over time. Reinvesting earnings creates additional returns on the initial investment as well as the accumulated interest.

Establishing an emergency fund provides a financial safety net, protecting against unforeseen expenses. This fund ensures that people may weather financial crises without jeopardizing their long-term wealth-building goals.

Real estate investment is a practical and historically established method of wealth building. Property ownership, rental income, and property appreciation all play an important role in long-term financial success.

TAX PLANNING
Understanding and optimizing tax techniques can increase total wealth. Using tax-advantaged investment vehicles and taking advantage of available deductions help to preserve more of one's profits.

Financial plans should be dynamic, adjusting to changes in personal circumstances, economic situations, and investment landscapes on a continuous basis. Reviewing and changing tactics on a regular basis assures their relevance and efficacy.

These ideas create a complete framework for successful wealth creation. Individuals can negotiate the complexity of wealth development with confidence and resilience by incorporating these guiding concepts into financial strategy.

Building wealth is a goal that many individuals strive for, yet it can often appear to be a daunting endeavor. It takes time, work, and discipline to achieve this goal, so don't be swayed by get-rich-quick schemes and too-good-to-be-true offers that can lead you astray.

The good news is that there are ideas and practices that can assist anyone in building and preserving money over time. And, the sooner you put things into action, the better your odds of success.

Setting goals and forming a strategy, investing in education and skills, managing debt, saving and investing, protecting your assets, recognizing the impact of taxes, and building a firm foundation are all critical elements for generating wealth.

KEY LESSONS

Following three fundamental actions and sticking to them is the key to building wealth over time.
The first stage is to generate enough money to satisfy your basic necessities while also saving some.
The second step is to control your spending in order to maximize your savings.
The third stage is to diversify your money by investing it in a range of various assets throughout time.

1. Make Money

The first thing you must do is begin earning money. This stage may appear simple, yet it is the most important for people who are just getting started. You've probably seen graphs that show how a small amount of money saved on a regular basis and allowed to compound grows over time.

There are two fundamental ways to earn money: earned income and passive income. Earned money is earned from your job, whereas passive income is derived from investments. You might not have any passive income until you have enough money to start investing.

If you are about to begin a career or considering a career change, the following questions may help you decide what you want to do—and where your earned income will come from:

What do you like to do? Doing something you enjoy and find significant will help you perform better, develop a longer-lasting career, and increase your chances of financial success. In fact, according to one study, more than nine out of ten workers claimed they would.

What do you excel at? Examine your strengths and how you may put them to use to make a living.
What will be profitable? Consider occupations that allow you to pursue what you love while also meeting your financial goals. The yearly Occupational Outlook Handbook produced by the U.S. Bureau of Labor Statistics is a valuable source of wage information as well as growth forecasts for numerous industries.

Investing in your education and talents is a fantastic approach to enhance your earning potential. Acquiring advanced academic degrees, industry-specific certifications, and training programs are all beneficial in terms of increasing your human capital.

2.Develop a plan and set goals

What will you do with your wealth? Do you wish to fund your retirement, or maybe retire early? Pay for your children's college education? Considering purchasing a second home? Do you want to give your money to charity? Setting goals is an important first step in accumulating wealth. When you have a clear vision of what you want to accomplish, you can devise a strategy to assist you get there.

Begin by identifying your financial objectives, such as saving for retirement, purchasing a home, or paying off debt.

 After you've determined your objectives, you should devise a strategy for reaching them. Creating a budget to help you save more money, improving your income through education or professional promotion, or investing in assets that will appreciate in value over time are all examples. Your strategy should be long-term, practical, and flexible. Review your progress on a regular basis and make adjustments as needed to stay on target.

3. Conserve funds

Making money will not help you grow wealth if you spend it all. Furthermore, if you don't have enough money saved up for your immediate commitments (such as bills, rent, or mortgage) or an emergency, you should prioritize saving above everything else. Many experts advise having several months'.

Consider the following actions to save more money for wealth creation:

- ❖ Keep a spending log for at least a month. You could use a financial software package to assist you with this, but a simple, pocket-sized notebook will suffice. Record all of your expenses, no matter how minor; many individuals are startled to find where all of their money goes.

❖ Find and remove the excess fat. Divide your spending into needs and wants. The obvious needs are food, shelter, and clothing. Add health insurance premiums to that list, as well as auto insurance if you own a car and life insurance if you support others. Many other expenses will be purely speculative.

❖ Set a savings target. Once you've determined how much money you can save each month, strive to keep to it. This does not imply that you must always live like a miser or be thrifty. If you're hitting your savings objectives, feel free to treat yourself with a small spend every now and then. You'll feel better and be more determined to continue on your path.

❖ Make saving automated. One simple way to save a predetermined amount each month is to have your company or bank transfer a portion of each paycheck into a separate savings or investing account. Similarly, you can save for retirement by having money deducted automatically from your paycheck.

❖ Discover high-yield savings. Shop for savings accounts with the best interest rates and lowest fees to maximize the payout of your savings. Certificates of deposit (CDs) are a fantastic way to save money if you can afford to lock it up for several months or years.Keep in mind that you can only save so many costs. If your expenses are already at a bare minimum, you should look at ways to improve your income.

4. Make an investment

Once you've saved some money, the next step is to invest it so that it can grow. Saving money is crucial, but the interest rates credited on deposit accounts are often relatively low, and your money risks losing purchasing value due to inflation over time.Diversification is perhaps the most crucial investing idea for novices (or any investor, for that matter). Simply put, your goal should be to distribute your funds among several sorts of assets.

This is due to the fact that investments perform differently at different times. For example, if the stock market is losing ground, bonds may offer attractive returns. If Stock A is down, Stock B could be on a roll.

Because mutual funds invest in a wide range of securities, they provide some built-in diversification. And if you invest in both a stock fund and a bond fund (or multiple stock funds and several bond funds), for example, rather than simply one or the other, you will obtain better diversification.

Another general guideline is that the younger you are, the more risk you can take because you will have more years to make up for any losses.

CHAPTER 2: THE FOUNDATION OF WEALTH BUILDING

"What is the first thing I should invest in?" is one of the most frequently asked questions at Wealth Builders. Our response is always the same: you! Whether you start with $500 or $1,000, you should invest in yourself before investing in assets.

The reason is straightforward. People are eager to begin their wealth-building path, yet impatience leads to errors. You have no idea what you don't know. If you start investing with $1,000 before doing your homework, you will spend more money than necessary.

Understanding the risk and reward is essential for any smart investing strategy. Then you do everything you can to reduce the risk and maximize the profit. When you invest in yourself, you increase your chances of success.

What does it mean to put money into yourself?
Time, knowledge, and money are three fundamental components of wealth creation. If you don't have much money (as many first-time investors do), you'll need to spend more time and knowledge to your wealth-building approach.

Investing in oneself entails devoting time to gaining financial knowledge. A consistent diet of books, podcasts, wealth-building courses, and mentors will assist you in increasing your financial knowledge.

Life long learners are successful investors. That is why investing in yourself is the cornerstone of wealth creation. If you're feeling stuck in your financial journey, it's time to invest in yourself by learning a new skill.

The nice thing is that regular and deliberate investing will result in a return. To Put It Simply, everything you spend your time and focus into will develop. As you spend more in yourself, your knowledge will grow. Here are three tips for investing in yourself.

Three Ways to Invest in Yourself

1. Assess Current Knowledge
Now is the time to be really truthful with yourself. Do you know the foundations of money development or do you need a refresher? Before venturing into deeper seas, it is necessary to have a solid financial base. Evaluating your current financial habits is an important part of self-investment.
For example, prior to investing, you should:

Get rid of your consumer debt.
Make and stick to a budget.
Create a safety net
Purchase a personal residence
These are only guidelines, and you can begin experimenting with investing before any of these are completed. However, if you're serious about getting started with wealth creation, here are some reasonable standards to aim toward.

Once you've established your financial basis, investing in yourself appears to be paid experience. Rather than squandering all of your investment funds on courses and books, it's time to get in the game and purchase an asset (something that grows in value over time). Finding your niche can help you with this.

put money into yourself

2. Identify Your Niche
After investing in yourself by learning fundamental financial principles, you can progress to studying specialized types of investing. You may be intimidated as a novice. If this is you, I have good news: there aren't a million ways to generate wealth--there are only a few!

Choose one or two areas in which you excel or desire to learn more.

This was my strategy for real estate investing. When I was in my forties, I learned that if I cash-flowed $300 each month on a set number of homes, I could replace my whole earned income. As a result, I set out to learn everything I could about real estate investing. When the moment came, I jumped in and started buying properties.

Here's the point: rather than attempting to be a jack of all trades, select a focus and master it.

put money into yourself

3. **Contribute to Your Community**
God intended for us to grow together. We learn best as a group. Information is useful, but impartation is superior! One of the best ways to invest in yourself is to surround yourself with people who support you.

If your network is prone to financial frivolity, that doesn't mean you have to fire everyone. However, you must be resilient in the face of financial comparison. Don't try to keep up with the Joneses if your buddies are buying pricey trips and nice dinners they can't afford on credit. Pray for divine connections and keep an eye out for the proper people to cross your path. Participate in growth environments such as networking groups and conferences. If you're feeling stuck in your financial journey, now might be a good moment to employ a coach.

When you invest in yourself, you will reap the benefits. Adding value to oneself brings value to others, transforming us into greater servants and stewards of all God's benefits.

Setting Financial Goals

Financial Setting goals is critical for financial success. If you're saving for a down payment on a new Asset or hope to retire early, having a strategy in place will help you get there as soon as possible.

Setting financial goals can help you save money, give you direction and purpose, and keep you on track to financial success. Setting financial goals can also motivate and excite you because it provides tangible indicators of progress.

Among other things, you may decide that your financial goal is to save for retirement, pay off debt, or invest in assets. Setting a financial goal is the first step in significantly improving your income.

Anyone with the courage to establish big financial objectives and design a plan to reach them can realize their financial dreams. The trick is to start small and work your way up. Set short-term financial goals first, then progress to greater financial goals.

Make it a habit to track your progress so you can adjust your plans as needed. You can reach enormous financial goals if you have the confidence to set them and apply yourself correctly - just take it one step at a time.

The Benefits of Setting Financial Goals
One of the most significant advantages of setting financial goals is that it allows you to stay focused and motivated. It is advantageous to have an end goal in mind.

Setting goals also gives you focus and direction. You know what you want and can plan your efforts accordingly. This provides for more efficient spending by allowing you to prioritize what must be done first and what can wait. It also makes it easier to stay organized because all of your plans are written out in front of you. Finally, goal setting increases your chances of success by forcing you to plan ahead of time and anticipate potential roadblocks.

Setting Effective Financial Objectives

Effective goal setting necessitates specificity, measurability, and timeliness. You must be explicit about your goals so that there is no space for misinterpretation or doubt later on.

The bottom line is that setting financial goals is one of the most effective ways for high-income workers to achieve long-term financial success. Goal setting, when done effectively, provides clarity and direction while remaining focused on the desired outcome; it encourages discipline by rewarding accomplishment; and, most importantly, it motivates during difficult times when progress may feel impossible or slow. By following these simple rules for effective goal planning, high earners can ensure that their money works hard for them rather than against them.

Budgeting and Saving Strategies

Budgeting is a fundamental skill that allows people to get control of their resources and work toward financial objectives. A budget allows you to keep track of your income and expenses, identify opportunities for savings, and make wise financial decisions.

In this book, we'll look at some simple and effective budgeting strategies that will help you save money and improve your financial status.

1. **Maintain a Record of Your Expenses:**Begin by recording one month's expenses. Keep track of all purchases, no matter how tiny. This will provide you a clear picture of where your money is going and will help you find excessive spending that may be reduced or eliminated.

2. **Set financial objectives:**Set clear financial objectives that you want to achieve. Having clear goals, whether it's saving for a vacation, paying off debt, or building an emergency fund, will drive you to stick to your budget and save money.

3. **Distinguish between wants and needs:**Distinguish between your wants and your necessities. Needs include things like food, shelter, and transportation, whereas desires are things you want but can live without. Prioritize your necessities and budget accordingly, while keeping your wants in check.

4. **Make a Budget That Is Realistic:**Create a realistic budget based on your monitored expenses and financial goals. Set a budget for each item, such as groceries, utilities, transportation, and entertainment. Make sure your spending don't surpass your revenue.

5. **Apply the 50/30/20 Rule:**Set aside 50% of your earnings for necessities, 30% for discretionary expenditure, and 20% for savings and debt reduction. These percentages should be adjusted based on your financial objectives and priorities.

6. **Automate Your Savings:**Set up a monthly transfer from your checking account to a separate savings account. You won't be tempted to squander the money this way, and it will grow slowly over time.

7. **Cut Unnecessary Spending:**Determine where you can reduce your spending. Examine your subscriptions, dining habits, and impulse purchases. To save money, consider alternatives such as cooking at home, canceling unwanted subscriptions, and purchasing inexpensive things.

8. **Price Comparison While Shopping:**Compare prices from many sellers before making a large buy. Look for special offers, discounts, or promotional codes. You may save money and get the best value for your money by conducting your homework.

9. **Examine and Modify Your Budget**Review your budget on a regular basis and keep track of your progress. Make changes as needed, especially if your financial circumstances or goals change. Budgeting is a fluid process, so be adaptable and change your techniques as needed.

Conclusion

Effective budgeting practices are essential for saving money and establishing financial security. You may gain control of your finances by tracking your expenses, setting objectives, separating needs from wants, developing a realistic budget, and automating saves. Budgeting is a lifelong skill that demands discipline and dedication.

Emergency Fund Essentials

Did you know that roughly a quarter of all adults in the United States have no emergency savings and only a quarter have a rainy day fund – with insufficient funds to cover even three months' worth of living expenses?

That means that almost 75% of the population is one emergency away from a true financial disaster.

Many people argue that their regular expenses and debt prevent them from saving for an emergency. An emergency fund, on the other hand, is one of the most effective debt-reduction measures. Having emergency funds on hand can prevent you from incurring further debt on a credit card.

Let's make sure you're prepared for a wet day.

Your Savings Guideline
While creating an emergency fund is a good idea for anybody, the amount you need to save will depend on your specific scenario.

"It depends on many different circumstances," but the most popular response from financial advisors is to save three to six months' worth of spending."

In the event of a job loss, for example, two-income households may be able to function on three months of savings, whereas one-income households and self-employed individuals may need to save closer to six months of income.

Your Emergency Fund Is Easily Accessible
The concept of saving for an emergency fund may be intimidating to you. Making a plan to help free up funds and speed up the process can make a significant difference.

Here are four strategies for using your current financial plan to develop an emergency fund.

1. Begin small and work your way up to $1,000. While you're trying to save for your larger emergency fund, it's critical to keep a little amount of money in the bank. This money can assist you in staying out of debt when you encounter inevitable roadblocks (for example, an appliance breaking down or an emergency visit to the doctor).

2. Credit card prices should be renegotiated. Ideally, you should prioritize debt repayment over savings growth. Try negotiating a lower interest rate on your credit cards to get an early start on establishing an emergency fund. Lowering your interest rate allows you to accelerate your debt-reduction efforts.Increase your auto insurance deductible.

3. Once your savings have reached a comfortable level to assist you in a minor emergency, such as changing tires on your vehicle, request a larger deductible from your car insurance carrier, which may lower your car insurance bill. You can add your monthly savings to your emergency fund.

4. Increase your savings rate over time. To accumulate enough funds to support you in a serious emergency, such as losing your work, it's a good idea to do more than just save your money – invest it. The goal is to keep your "job replacement" emergency fund distinct from the rest of your assets, where it may generate interest while you save it.

CHAPTER 3: UNDERSTANDING THE POWER OF REAL ESTATE

Understanding the counter-intuitive concepts of power is critical for success in modern culture. Change, information, mass, and control are all sources of power. You can sell your time, which is when you use your energy to get a specific result (which means you generate change). You may potentially have unique information that is valuable to others. You can gain power by exchanging that information for something of worth.

REAL ESTATE
The Real Powers Of Real Estate

You can also own a physical object with useful, valued properties (mass) and trade those properties for power or influence over time while still owning that object. You can also let your possession gain worth over time before trading it for power. This is where real estate enters the picture. Owning and managing it can offer you enormous power. Real estate represents the objects with the greatest literal mass that can exist on this planet.

Finally, you can wield authority over a big number of people, or even over someone with power. This is the power of control, and it is the most volatile, fleeting, and elusive sort of power. But it's really real, and it's the most powerful power of all — for as long as it lasts.

Celebrity is probably one of the best examples of power that comes from influence over people's thinking. Celebrity power is so appealing and prized in our society that we can see persons with tangible power of other forms taking huge action to achieve celebrity. The most well-known example is that of real estate mogul and Ex U.S. President Donald Trump. Initially known for his strength and influence in real estate and city development, he then chased the added power of celebrity, becoming a showman and, finally, President of the United States. Business titans such as Richard Branson, Elon Musk, and Jeff Bezos all court the media and develop their celebrity status in the same way.

That is why I find it fascinating to see how many entertainment and sports celebrities today make concerted efforts to move in the opposite direction, relying on the wise strategy of channeling their power and transforming it from the transient and erratic power of celebrity into the far more stable power of owning valuable properties. These clever, well-informed celebrities engage in real estate after amassing influence.

Serena Williams, for example, is not only a 23-time Grand Slam champion; she's also a wise real Estate investor, having made wise real estate purchases in Manhattan, Beverly hills, and Paris. Taylor Swift not too long purchased three houses in Manhattan's Tribeca area, one of which she purchased from another powerful-celebrity,
Peter Jackson is a well-known film director. Leonardo DiCaprio, an actor, producer, and environmentalist, is also well-known for his interest in eco-friendly real estate in Greenwich Village and Battery Park City.

But you don't have to be a celebrity to invest in Manhattan real estate. You don't even have to be wealthy; merely being financially secure and having a reliable team of real estate investing specialists will help you amass the power that comes with buying and selling properties.

Manhattan real estate is one of the most liquid markets in the country. It is determined by Wall Street's ups and downs, the wages and bonuses of the most influential consumers, changes in international buyer intentions, mortgage interest rates, the ability to obtain a mortgage, supply and demand, and other factors.

Real estate trends are constantly shifting, and the next six months might bring significant changes to the NYC market.

Whether you want to buy, renovate, and sell in a year or maintain a property for three to five years, New York real estate is for you. But, if you want to get the most out of New York real estate, my advice, based on decades of experience, is to buy and hold for at least five years. This allows you to catch large waves of buyers' and sellers' markets and considerably increase your earnings.

When it comes to exiting an investment, I believe that exchange is always the best option. Change up your portfolio: Invest in multifamily, mixed-use, retail, hotels, garages, self-storage, warehouses, and industrial assets, as well as residential and commercial properties. New York, fortunately for local investors, has it all.

Real Estate as a Wealth-Building Asset

Because it is uncorrelated to equities and bonds, real estate is well known for adding diversification to an investment portfolio. Real estate, on the other hand, adds far more to an investment portfolio and is one of the few asset sectors that may help investors establish generational wealth.

There are several ways that investors can use to grow wealth through real estate, each with its own set of benefits that can help you achieve your long-term objectives. According to a CNBC poll, nearly 25% of US citizen believe that real estate is the best way to earn wealth, outperforming equities, business ownership, and side hustles.

There are numerous advantages to investing in real estate. Given its independence from stocks and bonds, as well as its moderate volatility, real estate is one of those markets that can increase an investor's risk-reward exposure while also generating wealth for people and families over time.

Furthermore, real estate might also protect an investor's capital in a high-inflation economy like the one we are currently experiencing. Real estate can preserve an investor's capital gains through tax efficiency, in addition to increasing wealth. It may take time and a winning approach, but real estate investing can help you acquire the wealth you need for more financial freedom if you strike the perfect combination.

Wealth building is a notion that refers to earning long-term revenue through numerous channels other than a salary. Instead, wealth creation is a method of achieving financial independence that not only affects one's life but also the lives of future generations. Real estate is an important source of wealth creation, whether you are a newbie or a seasoned investor.

Real Estate Investment Financing
When investing in real estate for wealth creation, one of the most crucial considerations you'll have to make is how you'll fund your investment. The kind of real estate asset you Chase will have an impact on the type of financing you are likely to obtain.

Beginner residential property investors may purchase their first house with a Federal Housing Administration (FHA) loan, with the down payment varying depending on the property's valuation. Because the housing authority backs this loan, a lender can feel confident in offering the borrower a lower interest rate.

If it's a multi-family residence, you can live in one section for free while collecting rent on the other floors or sides. Ideally, your rental revenue should exceed any mortgage or mortgage insurance payments, providing you with some cash flow.

Of course, cash is still king in real estate. So, if you can pay for your property in full up front, you'll save money because you'll be saving the seller time. Surprisingly, there are certain hazards to buying real estate with cash.

For example, if you pay cash, your prospective returns are more limited than if you use finance. According to a Forbes article, you may make $10
50,000 by investing in a home and then renting it out for $2,000 per month.This will yield gross profits of $24,000 annually, a 9.6% gross return on your investment

However, if you put $50,000 down on the same house and get a 5% mortgage, you'll be paying $1,000 a month on that property. Renting it for the same $2,000 and deducting the mortgage payments results in an annual gross revenue of more than $12,200, resulting in a 25% gross return on your $50,000 down costs.

Conclusion
Real estate is one of the most common techniques to develop generational wealth, and it's not going away. If you are interested in expanding your investment portfolio and have prepared to persist with it for the long term, real estate has been shown for creating larger returns than other asset classes, leading to more financial freedom.

There are several other ways to invest, such REITs, private funds, rental properties, among others. And you can seek the form of financing that is best suited to your needs, whether it is a bridge loan, an FHA loan, or something else. The idea is to align your long-term financial objectives with your real estate investing strategy and risk/reward profile. Then, for future generations of people, focused on wealth creation.

Historical Success Stories

Introduction
Everyone comprehended California real estate was in a frothy bubble back in 2006. That is why we urged our RealWealth members to SELL California real estate and exchange it for homes in more affordable markets.

Whatever prompted us assume it was a bubble?

Simply put, affordability. Without the help of insane stated-income or negative amortization loans, the average California could not afford the average property in 2006. Those loans, of course, would inevitably adjust, and the borrower would be reluctant to make the higher payment.

I advised a woman who owned three homes in California at the time to sell and exchange them for properties in Dallas, a city in Texas. At the time, Dallas real estate was undervalued by 26%. In fact, unlike in California, incomes were increasing far faster than property values.

She complied to my advise and sold each Stockton property at a price of $420,000, enabling her to exchange them for nine cash flow real estate in Dallas.

She had been collecting $1200 in rent on her California properties and was ecstatic to learn she could get the same rent on her new properties, thus doubling her monthly income! This providing her with the extra funds she required to retire.

Remember that the California properties were ancient, in high-crime neighborhoods, and in desperate need of repair. The Dallas properties were brand new, in middle-class communities near decent schools and high-paying jobs.

When the credit crisis occurred a few years later, the Stockton properties she sold were worth approximately $100,000 each. in place of

She quadrupled her monthly income and saved her nest egg while losing a quarter of her net value.

Real Estate Investors has been assisting thousands of investors around the country in understanding market cycles in order to avoid tragedy and develop long-term wealth.

Continue reading to learn about 6 REAL success stories from real estate investors we've assisted.

Successful Story to No. 1
Sandra: Inform me about it. In just six months, I went from having no money to earning two thousand dollars a month.
Sandra, one of our members, acquired a home in San Francisco that was in disrepair and required extensive maintenance. It was essentially a take down, but it was still worth $500,000 (yep, San Francisco prices...)

Sandra decided to list it for a price of $1.3 million this summer to see whether she'd get an offer. She and her husband received an ALL-CASH offer for $1.45 million and closed in 10 days!

While this was amazing it also meant they had 45 days to find new houses or face massive capital gains. They had fortunate been attending Real Wealth events and listening to weekly market updates.

Real Estate Investors explores the country for affordable markets that have both job and population growth. Once places like this have been found identified, we look for the best real estate firms that can provide our members with turn-key properties.

The term "turn-key" refers to a real estate organization that buys a property at a bargain, renovates it to a like-new condition, finds a qualifying tenant, and provides ongoing property management.

.

They couldn't believe it when they discovered they could exchange their Single San Francisco property for 20+ cash flow properties... and their monthly passive income grew from zero to $20,000!

Success Story No. 2
Simon Allen explains how He purchased 13 properties that pay him $7,236 every month.

I met with our financial planner approximately a year ago, and he asked about our goals. "You know, we've raised a large family in California," I explained. We enjoy traveling and doing enjoyable stuff. I'd like to keep doing that, but I'm not sure how we'll be able to once we stop working. In fact, we're not sure we'll ever be able to retire!"

"My suggestion is to invest in annuities and safe bonds," he stated just before he sat down with all of our charts.

I considered how much money our financial advisor needed up front and how little we'd get in return. And we wouldn't get it until we were 80 years old! This was not a viable strategy.

Three weeks later, I was jogging on the treadmill alongside a friend who has done a lot of real estate investing. "Fourteen," he reacted when I asked how many properties he now owned.

"Are you kidding?" I exclaimed. How have you been so sure of yourself? Aren't you concerned that it might not be the perfect time, location, price, or whatever?"

"No, I'm really not," he said. "I've had a lot of success with it in Real Estate Investors.

Finally, historical success stories in wealth creation through real estate offer as great inspirations and vital lessons for those just starting out on their own financial adventures. These stories highlight numerous crucial points:

1. Resilience in Adversity: Many success stories feature people who overcame obstacles and disappointments by demonstrating resilience and tenacity. These anecdotes emphasize the necessity of sticking to long-term goals in the face of adversity.

2. Making Strategic Decisions: Successful people frequently made strategic decisions, whether it was discovering profitable real estate prospects, timing the market, or reacting to changing economic conditions. These decisions demonstrate the importance of informed and deliberate choices in wealth generation.

3. Diversification Techniques: Diversifying real estate investments or combining them with other asset types aided in achieving long-term profitability. These examples highlight the importance of a well-rounded and diverse education.

CHAPTER 4: STRATEGIES FOR REAL ESTATE INVESTMENT

What is Strategies for Real Estate Investing Entail?
The numerous ways and tactics that investors employ to make profits through the acquisition, ownership, management, and sale of properties are referred to as real estate investing strategies.

Based on parameters such as time horizon, risk tolerance, and projected return on investment, these techniques might differ dramatically.

Understanding and implementing the proper real estate investing plan is critical for investors to achieve success in the property market.

A well-defined strategy enables investors to make well-informed choices reduce risks, and optimize returns while aligning their investments with their financial objectives and market conditions.

Types of Strategies for Real Estate Investing

1. Long-Term Investing:

Long-term buy-and-hold entails purchasing a property and holding it for a longer period of time, often renting it out to create consistent rental income. This technique is based on the property's appreciation over time, which frequently results in considerable capital gains when the property is sold.

The fundamental benefit of the buy-and-hold approach is the possibility of long-term wealth accumulation. Investors can benefit from both ongoing rental income and capital appreciation as property values rise over time.

Additionally, this strategy allows investors to take advantage of various tax benefits, such as depreciation deductions and the potential for long-term capital gains tax rates.

2. Fix-And-Flip:

Fix-and-flip is a short-term real estate investing method in which an investor purchases a property that requires repairs or renovations, performs the necessary modifications, and then swiftly sells the property for a profit.

The goal is to reduce the holding period while increasing the return on investment.

For experienced investors with a sharp eye for discounted properties and great project management abilities, this technique can be successful.

It is, however, riskier than other tactics because it needs a considerable upfront capital commitment and there is always the danger of unanticipated expenses or a market collapse hurting resale value.

3. Wholesaling:

A real estate investing method in which an investor acts as a middleman between a property seller and a potential buyer is known as wholesaling.The investor buys the property at a low price and then assigns or sells the contract to another investor or end buyer at a higher price, making a profit in the process.

Because it often takes little to no money down, wholesaling can be an appealing approach for investors with low resources.To successfully wholesale homes, however, an in-depth knowledge of property valuations, negotiation skills, and a network of purchasers are required.

Furthermore, as compared to alternative methods, such as fix-and-flip or long-term buy-and-hold, this strategy often yields smaller profit margins.

4. Vacation Rentals on Airbnb:

The Airbnb/vacation rental method entails renting out a house to guests on a short-term basis, generally through platforms such as Airbnb or VRBO.

Because nightly rates tend to be higher and the property can be rented out year-round, this technique can provide larger rental income than standard long-term rentals.

Investing in Airbnb/vacation rentals necessitates careful thought of aspects such as location, property type, and local legislation.

Furthermore, because it includes dealing with regular guest turnover, cleaning, and upkeep, this technique might be more management-intensive.
It can, however, be extremely beneficial for those willing to put in the time and effort to efficiently manage their properties.

5. Commercial Property:

Commercial real estate investing entails the purchase and operation of commercial properties such as office buildings, retail complexes, and industrial facilities.

Because commercial leases typically have longer periods and higher rental rates than residential properties, this sort of investment can provide significant revenue possibilities.

Commercial real estate investing can be more complicated than residential real estate investing since it involves a greater understanding of market fundamentals, property management, and lease arrangements. It also usually necessitates a larger initial capital investment.

However, the prospect of consistent, long-term income and significant capital appreciation can make commercial real estate an appealing investment.

Factors to Consider in Choosing a Real Estate Investing Strategy

1. **Market Situation:**Market circumstances are critical in determining the success of any real estate investing strategy.To determine which tactics are most suited for the present market conditions, investors should carefully examine existing and future economic trends, local property valuations, and rental demand.Fix-and-flip or long-term buy-and-hold methods may produce larger returns in a rising market with significant demand for housing.In a softer market with lower property values and reduced demand, options such as wholesaling or focusing on rental income may be more appropriate.

2. **Location**: is crucial to the success of any real estate investment. When choosing a property and an investment strategy, investors must examine aspects such as local job growth, demographic trends, infrastructural advancements, and neighborhood amenities.Different sites may be more suited to specific techniques. Vacation rentals, for example, may be more profitable in famous tourist locations, whereas commercial real estate investments may perform better in places with high business activity.

3. **Capital:**The quantity of funds available to an investor will have a considerable impact on their choice of real estate investing strategy.Some tactics, such as fix-and-flip or commercial real estate investing, necessitate a significant initial investment for property acquisition and improvement.In contrast, alternatives such as wholesaling or Airbnb/vacation rentals may necessitate a lower initial investment.Investors should carefully evaluate their financial resources and select a strategy that fits their budget and long-term financial objectives.

4. **Tolerance for Risk:**The level of risk associated with various real estate investing strategies varies. When selecting an investment strategy, investors must examine their personal risk tolerance.Fix-and-flip investments, for example, can provide high profits but also carry the danger of unforeseen spending or market downturns, whereas long-term buy-and-hold investments are less hazardous but may provide lower short-term returns.

5. **Personal Objectives:**When selecting a real estate investing plan, an investor's personal goals and investment objectives should be considered.In Some investors may favor passive income and long-term wealth accumulation, whereas others may prioritize

short-term capital gains or portfolio diversification.Investors can increase their chances of success in the real estate market by matching their approach with their personal aspirations.

Research on How to Implement a Real Estate Investing Strategy

A good real estate investment strategy is built on thorough research. To identify potential opportunities and risks, investors should acquire information on market circumstances, property valuations, rental rates, and local legislation.
Online resources, local real estate brokers, and networking with other investors can all be good places to start.

1. **Set Objectives:**Setting specific, attainable goals is critical for staying focused and motivated during the real estate investing process.Short-term and long-term objectives, such as anticipated rental income, property value, or the number of properties to acquire within a given timeframe, should be established by investors.

2. **Form a Group:**Real estate investing frequently necessitates working with a variety of specialists, including real estate brokers, attorneys, property managers, and contractors.Putting together a solid team can help investors understand the complexities of the real estate market and have a more enjoyable investing experience.

3. **Ensured Funding:**Securing funding is a vital step in putting a real estate investing strategy into action.Investors should look into numerous financing choices, such as traditional mortgages, hard money loans, and private lending, and choose the best one for their plan and financial circumstances.

4. **Purchase the Property:** Once the financing is in place, investors can move forward with the purchase of the property. Negotiating with the seller, doing due diligence, and concluding the purchase through closing are all part of this process.

5. **Property Management:** Effective property management is critical for maximizing the profits on real estate investments. Investors should devise a strategy for maintaining the property, managing tenants, and dealing with any problems that arise.Investors may choose to manage the property themselves or employ a professional property management business, depending on their plan and personal preferences.

Conclusion

In summary, investors can choose from a variety of real estate investing strategies, including long-term buy-and-hold, fix-and-flip, wholesaling, Airbnb/vacation rentals, and commercial real estate.Each technique has its own set of benefits, problems, and risk considerations. Investors can choose the optimal method for achieving their goals by carefully examining market conditions, geography, capital, risk tolerance, and personal aspirations.For those that take the time to research, plan, and execute a well-defined strategy, real estate investing can be a satisfying and profitable enterprise.

It is critical to constantly review and modify the chosen approach in response to changing market conditions and personal circumstances.

Investors can establish a profitable real estate portfolio and reap the financial benefits by remaining informed, flexible, and focused on their goals.

Types of Real Estate Investments

What are considered the best real estate investments? With the U.S. real estate market on the rise, investors are sifting through every available property type to discover which will help them profit. So which sectors and properties are the best moves for investors today? Keep reading to learn more about the best type of real estate investment for you

Types of Real Estate Investments

Real estate investors should be familiar with terms such as commercial, residential, raw land, new development, crowdfunding platforms, and REITs. Each of these types will have unique advantages and disadvantages that investors should examine. Let's have a look at each of the alternatives:

Residential Property

Commercial Property

New Buildings and Undeveloped Land

REIT (Real Estate Investment Trusts)

Crowdfunding Websites

Diversification and risk management

1. Residential Real Estate
There are numerous sorts of rental properties in residential real estate, but single-family homes are thought to be the most popular. Other types of residential residences include duplexes, multifamily complexes, and holiday homes. Many investors choose residential real estate

because it produces a more consistent return. Of course, there are numerous residential real estate options.

Wholesaling, rehabilitating, and purchase and keep properties, all of which can create rental income, are the most prevalent exit strategies in residential real estate. Investors should undertake a thorough market research to determine which tactics would be most effective in their specific market location.

A residential real estate investment can be profitable if properly managed. This is because, in addition to providing consistent income flow, residential real estate benefits from a variety of tax savings.

2. Commercial Property

The best commercial assets to invest in are industrial, office, retail, hospitality, and multifamily developments. Commercial real estate investing can help investors that are dedicated about improving their communities.

Commercial buildings are regarded as one of the best types of real estate investments due to their potential for higher cash flow. Investors that choose commercial properties may discover that they offer more income possibilities, longer leases, and lower vacancy rates than other types of real estate. According to James Angel, co-founder of DYL, "industrial real estate includes warehouses, storage units, car washes, and other special-purpose properties that generate revenue from clients who visit the facility." Major fee and service revenue streams, such as coin-operated vacuum cleaners at a car wash, are typically included in industrial real estate acquisitions, which can assist the owner maximize their return on investment." Investors may also benefit from less competition in commercial real estate because buying these buildings might be a greater idea.

3. New Buildings and Undeveloped Land

Two sorts of real estate investments that can diversify an investor's portfolio are raw land investing and new construction. Raw land refers to any vacant land available for purchase, and it is particularly appealing in markets with significant growth potential. New building is not much different, but properties have already been erected on the land. In fast rising markets, investing in new development is also popular.

While many investors are inexperienced with raw land and new construction investing, both investments can provide lucrative returns. Whether you want to develop a property from the ground up or profit from a long-term buy and hold, raw land and new construction offer a unique opportunity for real estate investors.When investing in raw land and new building, investors should be prepared to conduct comprehensive market research in order to optimize earnings. This will ensure that you choose a desirable neighborhood and that the investment is not limited by market conditions.

4. **REITs (Real Estate Investment Trusts)**
Real estate investment trusts (REITs) are companies that own various forms of commercial real estate, such as hotels, stores, offices, malls, and restaurants. You can buy stock in these real estate companies. When you invest in a REIT, you are investing in the properties that these corporations own rather of taking on the risk of owning the property yourself.
REITs must return 90% of their taxable income to shareholders each year. As a result, investors can
 This allows investors to collect dividends while diversifying their portfolio. In addition, unlike other types of real estate investments, publicly traded REITs provide flexible liquidity. If you need emergency finances, you can sell your firm shares on the stock exchange.

5. **Crowdfunding Websites**
Crowdfunding platforms provide investors with access to a variety of high-return assets that have traditionally been reserved for the wealthy. While this provides investors with the convenience of accessing assets, it also brings a significant level of risk. Crowdfunding sites normally only accept accredited investors or individuals with a high net worth.Some sites also accept non-accredited investors.

The most common types of real estate investments made through crowdfunding platforms are non-traded REITs, or REITs that are not listed on a stock exchange. In the case of non-traded REITs, your cash may be invested for several years with no way to withdraw them when needed.

Summary
For investors willing to put in the effort, a variety of property kinds can produce substantial profit margins. However, with so many possibilities accessible, many investors are inclined to ponder what is the finest real estate investment. While this is a simple question, there is no simple response. Many considerations will determine the best form of investment property, and investors must be cautious When searching for potential transactions, rule out all choices.

CHAPTER 5: FINANCIAL PLANNING FOR LONG-TERM WEALTH

Our daily lives are like rollercoasters, having many ups and downs, and financial planning can help you smooth the ride. Whether you have only recently started your career or are in your 30s or 40s, financial concerns can arise from anyone, so having a strong financial plan to ensure your future is critical. Financial planning allows you to create a roadmap for your financial journey in order to attain your financial objectives.

This book will go over fundamental financial planning features, importance, and rewards. We will also go over the procedures for financial planning and how to construct your own plan to attain all of your goals.

What is financial planning?

Financial planning is the process of managing your financial resources in order to reach your long-term or short-term objectives. It comprises evaluating your existing financial condition, determining your financial goals and risk tolerance, and developing a strategy to accomplish them. It enables you to make informed decisions about how to manage your finances. Simply simply, financial planning assists you in keeping your finances under control in order to fulfill all of your goals and desires. To have a better understanding of financial planning, consider its various types, objectives, importance, and benefits.

Various types of financial planning

Financial planning is done to fulfill your long-term goals, such as investment, tax savings, retirement, education, and so on. Based on them, some popular methods of financial planning are:

1. **Investment Planning:** Investment planning involves developing plans for future investments. You can plan for the type and amount of investment you want. You can

deploy your cash to a variety of investment vehicles, including mutual funds, NPS, and ELSS.

2. **Tax Planning:** Financial planning can also help you resolve tax concerns. Tax planning involves developing financial solutions to reduce tax liabilities. Fixed deposits, NPS, PPF, ELSS, and other investment options can help you save the most money on taxes.

3. **Retirement Planning**: Strategies are developed to ensure that you retire richly. Retirement requires a large corpus to finance your lifestyle for 20-30 years, and retirement planning can help you achieve that. It helps you estimate the money you would . It will assist you in estimating the money required to retire and how much you should spend to make that happen.

4. **Budgeting:**is the process of analyzing your income and expenses and creating financial plans based on that information. It focuses on reducing expenses and debts while increasing your discretionary income.

5. **Insurance Planning:** Insurance offers financial aid in times of disaster. Insurance planning assists you in determining what type of insurance you need and how much coverage you should have.

6. **Educational funding planning:** As the cost of higher education in India has risen over the years, financial planning for education has become increasingly vital. Financial planning ahead of time for education fees ensures that you do not have to sacrifice your aspirations.Estate planning is a financial plan that allows you to smoothly transfer your possessions to your loved ones after your death. It aids in the avoidance of family feuds and arguments over who receives what.

7. **Estate Planning**:Making a will is an important element of estate preparation because it prevents family feuds over property or assets. It provides a road plan for the transfer of assets among family members following your death.

8. **Wealth creation**: Effective budgeting is one way that financial planning can help you create wealth. It lets you keep track of your income and expenses. You may increase your investment surplus by tracking your spending and eliminating unneeded expenses.You can invest this surplus in a variety of investment vehicles, including stocks.

Objectives of Financial Planning

Budgeting: Financial planning assists you in creating a personal budget that suits your financial plan. It allows you to keep track of your income and costs while minimizing them.

Determine your present financial position: Financial planning can assist you determine your current financial situation by analyzing your current income, expenses, and liabilities. It takes into account your long-term objectives and assists you in developing an investment strategy to meet them.

Setting Financial Goals: It assists you in identifying your financial goals. Retirement savings, home ownership or construction, education or marriage for children, and so on are examples of such ambitions.

Making financial plans: Making financial plans helps you to take action in order to attain your short- or long-term goals. It outlines the many investment strategies you might employ to reach your financial objectives.

Review financial plans: Your financial plans must be monitored on a regular basis to ensure that they are aligned with your goals. Financial planning assists you in reviewing your portfolio's performance.

Financial Planning: Importance and Benefits

Everyone has a long list of things they wish to do with their money. This could involve lowering taxes, purchasing the latest smartphone, laptop, car, and property, saving for children's education, retirement planning, and so forth.

However, more often than not, the money we have is insufficient to meet all of our needs. As a result, it is critical that we establish clear priorities. In this regard, financial preparation can be beneficial.

Financial planning is important because it guides us toward our goals. Financial planning helps you better understand your goals, including why you need to reach them and how they affect other elements of your life and finances. Furthermore, financial planning provides benefits such as a smoother transition into various life stages, being prepared for emergencies, better tax planning, and so on.

Let's go over the advantages of financial planning in depth.

Smoother Transition to Different Life Stages

As we progress through life stages, our priorities and duties shift. Financial planning teaches us how to manage our finances at various times of life, such as bachelorhood, marriage, and post-retirement.

Helps Stay prepared for emergencies.

Creating an emergency fund is an important part of financial planning. An emergency fund ensures that you have enough money to cover at least 9-12 months' worth of monthly costs. This way, you won't have to worry about money if you experience a family emergency, get a pay cut, or lose your work.

Helps Calculate the Right Insurance Term and health insurance provide valuable coverage in the event of an unexpected death.

Reasons for Financial Planning.

Financial planning is an essential component of any individual's life since it helps them achieve their goals, ensure their financial future, and offer financial stability. Here are some of the reasons to create a financial plan:

- ❖ It enables you to set financial goals, such as purchasing a home, a car, saving for children, and so on, and work toward those goals.

- ❖ It helps you construct a budget that allows you to cut wasteful costs, reduce debts, and improve your spare income.

- ❖ It's encourages regular saving and investment, allowing you to build a large corpus in the future by investing consistently.

- ❖ At retirement, you need a consistent source of income. You can establish a healthy retirement corpus, which will provide you with monthly income to cover your everyday expenses.

❖ It assists you in lowering your tax liability by directing your funds to various tax-saving investments.

Financial Planning Tips for Various Sections

Financial planning improves financial security and enables you to reach long-term financial goals.
So, whether you are a salaried individual planning for retirement or self-employed, everyone needs a solid financial strategy to ensure their future.

Learn how different individuals can create efficient financial planning for salaried employees. A solid financial plan is essential for salaried employees in order to meet their financial objectives.

Here are some suggestions for creating a decent financial plan:
  ❖ You can use a budget to track and manage your savings, expenses, and investments.
  ❖ Consider investing in mutual funds, which provide a diverse range of investments.
  ❖ Make sure you have health insurance for both yourself and your family for future expenses.

Financial Planning for Retirement

If you are planning for retirement, you should have proper financial planning in place to ensure that you receive continuous cash flow once you retire. Here are some suggestions for retirement planning:

- You could consider investing in the National Pension System (NPS). It is a market-linked investment that comprises a diverse range of asset classes. It provides the twin benefit of taxation and a regular annuity at retirement.

- If you do not want to incur bigger risks, you should choose PPF (Public Provident Fund). It is a government-backed tax saving initiative that provides a sure investment return.

To put it Simply,Financial planning is all about preparing a trip that will take you securely to your destination. In this blog, we discussed the significance of financial planning. We've also provided examples to help you understand how to approach financial planning. However, a written financial strategy is useless unless it is implemented.

Retirement Planning

What is Retirement Planning?
Retirement planning entails identifying retirement income objectives and what is required to accomplish them. Retirement planning entails determining income sources, estimating expenses, establishing a savings plan, and managing assets and risk. Future cash flows are predicted to determine whether the retirement income target is achievable.

You can begin at any moment, but it works best if you include it into your financial plan as soon as feasible. That's the best method to assure a safe, secure, and enjoyable retirement. The fun aspect is why it makes sense to focus on the serious, and sometimes boring, portion: figuring out how you'll get there.

How Retirement Planning Works
To put it simply, retirement planning is the process of preparing for life after paid labor. This applies to many facets of life, not just finances.

Non-financial components include lifestyle decisions such as how to spend retirement time, where to live, and when to stop working entirely, among others. All of these factors are taken into account in a comprehensive retirement planning strategy.

The emphasis on retirement preparation shifts as one progresses through life. For example:

Retirement planning begins early in a person's working life and focuses on saving enough money for retirement.
During the middle of your career, it may also include establishing specific income or asset goals and taking efforts to meet them.
When you reach retirement age, you transition from asset accumulation to distribution, as defined by financial planners. You are no longer contributing to your retirement account(s). Instead, your decades-long savings start paying you off.

Investment Portfolios

What is an Investment Portfolio?
An investment portfolio is the ownership of a stock, bond, or other financial instrument with the hope that it will generate a return or increase in value over time, or both. It comprises passive or hands-off ownership of assets, as opposed to direct investing, which requires active management.

Portfolio investment can be categorized into two major categories:

Strategic investing entails purchasing financial assets for their long-term growth potential, income yield, or both, with the goal of retaining them for an extended period of time.
The tactical method necessitates aggressive buying and selling in order to generate short-term profits.
Understanding Portfolio Investments
Portfolio investments span a wide range of asset classes, including equities and government.

KEY TAKEAWAYS
- A portfolio investment is an asset purchased with the hope that it would generate a profit or increase in value, or both.

- In contrast to direct investments, which need active management, portfolio investments are passive.

- Risk tolerance and time horizon are important considerations when picking a portfolio investment.

- Physical investments include real estate, commodities, art, land, timber, and gold.In truth, a portfolio investment can be any asset purchased with the intention of creating a return in the short or long term.

- Making choices.A variety of factors influence the composition of an investment portfolio. The most crucial factors are the investor's risk tolerance and investing time horizon. Is the investor a younger professional?

- Investors with a higher risk tolerance may favor growth equities, real estate, overseas securities, and options, whilst more conservative investors may prefer government bonds and blue-chip companies.

- On a wider scale, mutual funds and institutional investors make portfolio investments. Infrastructure assets such as bridges and toll roads may be included for the largest institutional investors, such as pension funds and sovereign funds.

- Institutional investors' portfolio investments are often long-term and conservative in nature. Pension and college endowment funds do not invest in speculative equities.

- Portfolio Investments For Retirement
  Investors investing for retirement are generally urged to diversify their portfolios using low-cost investments.

- Index funds are popular in individual retirement accounts (IRAs) and 401(k) plans because they provide broad exposure to a variety of asset classes at a low cost. These funds are excellent core holdings for retirement portfolios.Those who want a more hands-on approach can adjust their portfolio allocations by including real estate, private equity, and individual stocks and bonds.

Tax Planning

What is Tax Planning?

Tax planning is the examination of a financial condition or plan to ensure that all components work together to allow you to pay the lowest feasible taxes. Tax efficiency refers to a plan that minimizes the amount of taxes you pay. Tax preparation should be a key component of each individual investor's financial plan. Reduced tax liability and increased ability to contribute to retirement plans are critical for success.

KEY TAKEAWAYS
- Tax planning is the examination of a financial condition or plan to ensure that all components work together to allow you to pay the lowest feasible taxes.
- Tax planning considerations include income timing, size, purchase timing, and expenditure planning.
- Tax planning techniques can include putting money aside for retirement in an IRA or taking advantage of tax gains and losses.

Understanding Tax Planning.

Tax preparation involves a number of considerations. Considerations include the timing of income, the magnitude and timing of purchases, and budgeting for other expenses. To achieve the best results, the investment and retirement plan options must complement the tax filing status and deductions.

Retirement Savings Strategies

Saving in a retirement plan is a common approach to effectively cut taxes. Contributing money to a traditional IRA reduces gross income by the amount donated. For 2024, provided all conditions are met, a filer under the age of 60 can contribute up to $6,500 to their IRA, with an extra $1,000 catch-up contribution if they are 60 or older. That figure rises to $7,000 in 2025, but the catch-up contribution remains unchanged at $1,000.

Tax Planning Versus Tax Gain-Loss Harvesting.

Tax gain-loss harvesting is another type of investment-related tax planning or management. It is useful because it helps offset a portfolio's losses with overall capital gains. According to the IRS, short and long-term capital losses must first be utilized.

The IRS requires that short and long-term capital losses be used to offset capital gains of the same sort.
In other words, long-term losses cancel out long-term benefits before compensating for short-term gains. Short-term capital gains, or earnings from assets held for less than a year, are taxed at the regular income rate.

For example, if a single investor with a $100,000 income earned $10,000 in long-term capital gains, he or she would owe $1,500 in taxes. If the same investor sold failing investments with long-term capital losses of $10,000, the losses would negate the gains, resulting in a tax liability of zero. If the same losing investment was brought back, a minimum of 30 days would have passed to avoid suffering a wash.

CHAPTER 6: OVERCOMING CHALLENGES IN WEALTH BUILDING

Most people would agree that their primary financial goal is to become financially independent. Those who have already attained financial independence may change their goal to maintain that status. It is worthwhile to examine some of the biggest impediments to achieving those goals and determine how they might be overcome.

Spending and Saving

Saving is the process of deferring consuming in order to consume later. This differs from investing, which Warren Buffett defines as foregoing current spending in order to consume more later. The consequence of the definition is intriguing. Not only must investors preserve the purchase power of their investments (i.e., their savings must earn at least Earn a return that is at least equal to the rate of inflation); they must grow their purchasing power while overcoming the various other barriers to success.

The major barrier to gaining or maintaining financial independence is spending. There is little doubt that many consumers prioritize current consumption over future consumption. For a young family, home payments and the cost of raising and educating their children take precedence over saving for a distant retirement. And it's appropriate that they're ranked higher. However, a little financial preparation can assist determine the type of lifestyle that can be enjoyed now while maintaining the potential of future financial freedom.

Similarly, even someone who appears to have more than enough money to live comfortably for the rest of his or her life might easily lose that financial stability if it is not handled properly. Although maybe an extreme example, former professional hockey star Theo Fleury said in his autobiography Playing with Fire that he wasted more than $50 million earned throughout his playing career on liquor, drugs, and gambling. Clearly, avoiding alcohol, drugs, and gambling is a good idea, but the key is to understand what amount of spending is sustainable in your specific circumstances.

Taxes

Taxes are one of the largest annual expenses for most people, and they can happily do without them. In Canada, income taxes can be paid on up to 50% of earned income, depending on the amount and province of residency. For investors, the situation is slightly better because certain types of income (Canadian dividends, capital gains) are taxed at far lower rates. Furthermore, capital gains are taxed only after the property is sold and the capital gain is realized. Owning shares in high-quality companies that can be held for a long period is analogous to investing in an RRSP or RRIF, which are taxed only when funds are withdrawn.

When shares are purchased outside of an RRSP, there is no immediate tax benefit, but no tax is paid while they are owned (we're disregarding dividends for the sake of simplicity), and when they are finally sold, the gain is taxed at half the rate charged on an RRSP or RRIF exit.

There are numerous factors that influence an individual's tax liability, including the amount and source of income. While we typically think of taxes as a proportion of income (e.g., the 50% indicated above), thinking of them as a percentage of one's portfolio might help put things in perspective.

Income tax on an investment portfolio typically ranges from ½% to 3½% of its value. Individuals with large yearly RRIF withdrawals, significant interest income, and regularly traded stock portfolios would fall in the upper half of the range, while individuals with no RRIF income, little interest income, and infrequently traded equities portfolios would fall in the bottom half.

Before you assume that we are discouraging the use of RRSP/RRIFs due to the high withdrawal tax rate, keep in mind that while the Canada Revenue Agency will eventually want to receive a portion of your RRSP contributions and investment gains, your investment returns are tax-sheltered and compounding over time.

Management Fees and Other Investment Costs

It's difficult to pick up the newspaper's personal finance pages without encountering another column about the negative impact of investing fees on net investment returns. We at Genova get fees for managing investment accounts, thus we are far from objective in this regard. However, like with any other expense, we believe that the quantity paid is less essential than the value gained in return.

Except for stuffing cash in one's mattress, no investment has no expense, either directly or indirectly. Even depositing into a bank savings account involves the indirect cost of the disparity between what the bank pays you in interest and what it earns when it lends your money to somebody else. In a more diverse portfolio, costs include transaction fees for buying and selling investments, custodial charges for keeping investments secure, collecting investment income, arranging payment for purchases, and collecting sales profits. Even do-it-yourself investors will face these expenses, albeit they may be included in a commission or administration fee.

There is an additional cost for an individual who wants to delegate the functions of investment research (essentially, determining what companies to own and what to pay for them) and portfolio management (applying the results of investment research to individual portfolios in order to achieve defined goals).
The pundits are accurate that paying a high fee for managing a portfolio that matches an index makes little sense when the same result can be acquired at a considerably lower cost. We believe there is significant value in continuously sensible investing research and portfolio management that reflects established financial goals. However, it is ultimately up to the client to evaluate whether the value received is sufficient for the price paid.

Inflation

Inflation is undoubtedly the most subtle destroyer of investment profits. Remember that investing is defined as spending less now in order to consume more tomorrow. However, having more money does not necessarily mean you can eat more.
Interestingly, if you had purchased one-year GICs that paid an average of 1.3% yearly interest and reinvested the interest received, you would have approximately $109 today (before taxes), which would not buy you what $90 could have bought seven years ago.

Navigating the Obstacle Course

Those who desire to acquire or retain financial independence must overcome the hurdles that stand in their way. One must save and invest enough to gain independence, or spend only what is necessary to maintain existing riches. One must also earn enough to pay taxes on investment earnings and cover the costs of acquiring them. If we estimate that the combined effect of inflation, taxes, and costs will erode a portfolio's value by 4%-6% per year, it is clear why investments held in excess of those required for liquidity must be growth-oriented. While it is always worthwhile to look for ways to reduce taxes and other expenses, the primary goal should be to get a solid return.

When constructing the growth component of a portfolio, it is also critical to avoid another hazard that we have not before mentioned: speculating. Investing in junior resource exploration firms or high-tech startup enterprises, for example, a result in a windfall or a painful learning experience.

Common Pitfalls and How to Avoid Them

When it comes to real estate deals, knowledge is key. Understanding the common problems that can occur during the process can help you avoid costly blunders and ensure a smooth and successful purchase. In this post, we'll look at the most prevalent problems in real estate transactions and offer helpful advice on how to prevent them. Whether you're a buyer or a seller, being aware of these traps will allow you to confidently navigate the complex world of real estate and make informed decisions.

I. Lack of proper research and due diligence.

1. The significance of extensive investigation before getting into a transaction.

Before entering into a real estate deal, it is critical to undertake extensive research. This includes acquiring information on the property and its history.

2. Conducting title searches and property inspections.

One common error is failing to conduct title searches and property inspections. A thorough title check guarantees that the property you're interested in is free of liens, encumbrances, and legal challenges. Furthermore, engaging a professional inspector to thoroughly examine the property's condition can reveal hidden issues that may influence your decision to proceed with the acquisition.

3. Evaluate the property's location and future development plans.

The location of a property influences its value and potential for future growth. Consider the neighborhood's reputation, crime rates, closeness to amenities, and transportation options. Furthermore, be updated about any future development plans in the region, as these can affect the property's appeal and value over time.

II. Insufficient Financial Planning.

1. Assessing affordability and creating a budget

One of the most important aspects in any real estate deal is assessing your affordability. Evaluate your financial condition, including your income, expenses, and current debts. Create a realistic budget that includes not only the purchase price but also other expenses like as taxes, insurance, and upkeep.

2. Understanding the mortgage alternatives and terms.
If you need financing for a real estate acquisition, you should grasp the many mortgage choices accessible to you. Investigate various lenders, compare interest rates, and thoroughly examine the terms and conditions of each loan. Consult with a mortgage professional to find the best mortgage choice for your needs and financial situation.

3. Accounting for other costs like as taxes, insurance, and upkeep.
Many buyers underestimate the added expenditures of owning a property. Property taxes, homeowners insurance, and maintenance costs can have a big impact on your monthly budget. To avoid long-term financial pressure, make careful to account in these fees when considering the affordability of a house.

III. A lack of clear communication

1. Importance of efficient communication among all parties involved
Clear and honest communication is essential throughout the real estate transaction process. Create a line of communication between your real estate agent, attorney, mortgage lender, and any other parties involved. Timely and clear communication prevents misunderstandings and ensures that everyone is on the same page.

2. Keeping an open and honest discussion with real estate agents and attorneys.
Your real estate agent and attorney are helpful resources that can help you navigate the deal. Maintain open and honest contact with them, and express your expectations, concerns, and preferences. They can provide you competent guidance, answer your concerns, and help you make informed decisions.

3. Define expectations and criteria in writing.
To minimize misunderstandings and disagreements, all expectations and requirements should be explicitly established in writing. Make sure all agreements, proposals, and counteroffers are

in writing and signed by all parties involved. This protects your interests and creates a verifiable record of the transactions.

IV. Failure to Review and Understand Contracts.

1. The significance of checking all contracts thoroughly.
Real estate transactions include several legal paperwork and contracts. It is critical to thoroughly analyze them and obtain legal counsel if necessary. Pay particular attention to the terms, conditions, contingencies, and deadlines indicated in the contract. Examining contracts properly ensures that you understand your rights and obligations.

2. Seeking legal guidance whenever necessary.
Real estate transactions can be complex, and legal representation is frequently required to manage the complexities of the contracts involved. Use the services of a knowledgeable real estate attorney who specializes in the local market. They will assist you in understanding the legal ramifications, protecting your interests, and ensuring compliance with local rules.

3. Understand essential words, circumstances, and potential dangers.
Contracts include technical terms and contingencies that might have a substantial impact on the transaction. Take the time to grasp these words, and ask clarification if necessary. Be aware of any potential risks, such as finance contingencies, inspection contingencies, or specified timetables that may impact the transaction.

V. Neglecting Property Inspection and Appraisal Contingencies

1. The significance of introducing inspection and evaluation contingencies in contracts
Buyers are protected by the purchase contract, which includes inspection and appraisal contingencies. An inspection contingency permits you to thoroughly assess the property and negotiate repairs or price modifications if major faults are detected. An appraisal contingency assures that the property's valuation matches the agreed-upon purchase price.

2. Conducted a full property inspection.
A property inspection is an important stage in the due diligence process. Hire a skilled home inspector to evaluate the property's structural integrity, systems, and overall condition. Pay particular attention to any potential plumbing, electrical, roofing, or foundation issues. The inspector's findings will provide significant insight into the property's condition, allowing you to make an informed decision.

3. Understanding the appraisal procedure and its ramifications.
An appraisal is performed by a professional appraiser to assess the property's fair market worth. The appraisal guarantees that the property's valuation matches the loan amount sought by the buyer. Understanding the appraisal process and its ramifications is critical because it can impact the lender's decision and effect the financial transaction.

Conclusion
Real estate transactions can be complicated, but with proper planning and attention to detail, you can avoid typical mistakes and achieve a good end. A successful acquisition requires thorough study, good financial planning, effective communication, and an understanding of contracts. It is critical to be familiar with zoning requirements, HOA rules, insurance coverage, and market trends. Seeking competent advice and keeping correct paperwork during the procedure is also necessary. By avoiding these frequent traps, you may confidently navigate the real estate market and achieve your objectives.

Building Resilience in Financial Ventures

The anxiety that businesses experienced at the outset of the pandemic has returned, with many expecting a global slowdown. According to the Straits Times, over three-quarters of the World Economic Forum's Community of Chief Economists believe a worldwide recession is likely.

Several factors contribute to this unpredictability and market volatility, including supply and demand shocks, aggressive inflation-control efforts, and a lack of finance for new initiatives. These have an impact on capital flows and investment habits, notably in the technology sector. As a result, financial services organizations are using various strategies to adapt to the shifting market. These include plat formification and front-office digitalization to reduce operating expenses while offering new digital offerings.

In short, organizations face both an opportunity and a difficulty in reimagining their business models and client experiences.
Building new paths to success in financial services
Salesforce Customer 360 can assist businesses in navigating upcoming problems and identifying new possibilities. Salesforce's Financial Services Cloud provides a platform for financial institutions to establish trust. It integrates the customer experience across channels, locations, and lines of business for both consumer and commercial enterprises.

Financial services businesses may boost staff productivity, speed time to value, and deepen client trust with every encounter by leveraging purpose-built industry functionality and Sales Cloud and Service Cloud capabilities. More significantly, they can be present in the moment for their clients, who rely on and trust them with their financial affairs.

At the same time, MuleSoft enables businesses to simply automate any process in order to increase efficiency and productivity. MuleSoft also integrates many systems to improve the client experience.

Slack enables speedier issue resolution, which leads to higher levels of customer satisfaction. The strong collaboration tool also allows for seamless communication with partners and customers, resulting in less friction, increased innovation, and faster decision-making.

Embedded experiences and ecosystems support new business models easily.

Salesforce is a strong supporter of stakeholder capitalism and is dedicated to doing right by all of its stakeholders, including customers, employees, partners, communities, the environment, and society as a whole. And we believe that data and technology may help to create more robust and inclusive business models that meet the demands of all stakeholders in the financial services industry.

CHAPTER 7:REAL-LIFE EXAMPLES OF GENERATIONAL WEALTH CREATION

My Wife and I often discuss the things we want to teach our children and how we may help them succeed in life while also teaching them to be financially responsible individuals. One common theme is our ambition to generate generational wealth.

Why does generational wealth matter?

Wealth provides greater alternatives in life.
Generational wealth is significant because it gives you more freedom to think and live the life you want when you don't have to worry about paying expenses or whether you can afford to leave a job that doesn't satisfy you.

But why should you care about passing on money to the next generation? Many people have felt compelled to undertake something or work a job because They need the money.
Of course, generating generational wealth does not imply that your children will never face adversity. However, many parents want to give their children more alternatives in life.

Challenges of Creating Generational Wealth
Unfortunately, the default for parents is to work hard and pass on assets. However, that scenario is unlikely to work in most cases. That is why an estimated 70% of generational wealth is lost by the second generation, and 90% by the third.1
Most parents who came from low beginnings do not want their children to go through the same challenges they endured.

Here are a few strategies for creating generational wealth.

How to Build Generational Wealth

1. Support your child's education.
Raising financially independent adults is essential if you want to build long-term wealth.
Teaching your children about personal money can help them build a road to self-sufficiency.
Giving your children a financial education is one of the most critical things you can do to begin
accumulating generational wealth. It all starts with open conversations about money at home, so
your children understand they can ask questions.
In our household, we have age-appropriate daily conversations about money with our children
aged seven and under.

The topics range from need vs want to earning money to the value of saving and giving back.
Our 7-year-old has begun taking weekly financial literacy tests and learning about investing. As
our children grow older, we plan to introduce them to more advanced personal finance ideas. As
we learn more and discover new tools, we incorporate what we know into our children's
education.
Our goal is for them to be financially responsible individuals by the time they leave home as
young adults.
It can be scary to embark on that duty, especially if you're trying to figure out your money, but
most people learn from their mistakes rather than their accomplishments. The same goes for
money. Children can benefit from our financial successes,However, they might also benefit from
our financial blunders. As parents, we may be hesitant to discuss our failures and mistakes, but
by discussing our losses and what we learned from them, we can assist our children avoid
some of the same mistakes we did.

2. Invest in the stock market.
You can invest in a variety of assets. Signing up for Empower's free financial tools may help you
better understand your net worth, which is your assets minus your liabilities. Millions of
households in the United States utilize this technology to view all of their financial accounts and
analyze their investments for free.
Investing in the stock market allows you to develop wealth passively while protecting your
money from inflation.Investing in the stock market might be scary at first; therefore, as a novice,
a simple method to get started is through low-cost index funds, which provide long-term growth
prospects at comparatively modest costs.

3. Invest in Real Estate

Real estate can be an excellent way to acquire wealth. Real estate often appreciates over time. Real estate can also generate cash flow for investors.

It may be difficult to envision yourself as a real estate investor. However, there are less scary methods to get started, such as moving out of your house, renting it out, or buying another property. Many investors have adopted this technique to develop their real estate portfolios one house at a time.

4. Start a business to pass down.

More over 30% of family-owned enterprises are thought to have reached the second generation.3 Building a business to pass on to your offspring is another approach to create generational wealth. Anyone who wants to pass on their business to their kids should start working in it at a young age. It can assist motivate them to take over the organization in question. However, if your offspring are not interested in running the family business, there is still a way to generate income by selling it.

How to pass on generational wealth.

Creating an estate plan is a vital step in establishing generational wealth.It ensures that your assets are distributed in accordance with your preferences in the case of your death or incapacity.

There are various procedures that can be taken to ensure that money is passed down through generations. Here's a few.

1. Write a will.

A will should provide clear instructions on your final wishes and assets. Understanding the laws in your state is critical to ensuring that your will is valid. A will can also assist you communicate your wishes for your young children's care. You can also disclose your financial holdings to help your family members find them. When you do not have a will, the state decides what happens to your children, property, and possessions.

2. **Establish a trust.**
A trust, sometimes known as a trust fund, is a legal structure that you can employ to hold and transfer assets to your beneficiaries. It is another option to explore for parents with minor children. Trusts can be costly, but they can have other advantages, such as avoiding or decreasing estate and gift taxes based on the size of your estate.

3. **Name account beneficiaries.**
Naming specified beneficiaries for each account can often be enough to ensure that your assets pass down to the beneficiaries of your choice. Naming beneficiaries can save your loved ones time and energy after your death, especially if they are adults.

4. **Proper Estate Planning**
Proper estate planning is a critical component of passing on family wealth. As a result, consulting with an estate attorney is critical to ensuring that you have a comprehensive estate plan in place.

Bottom line.
Creating generational wealth is not an easy undertaking.
Beyond the difficult process of accumulating wealth, education and appropriate estate planning are two critical elements that we as parents must prioritize equally if we want the riches to last.

Lessons Learned from Successful Individuals

1. **They are willing to take risks:**Successful people take calculated risks, not simply random ones. They consider their risk exposure and measure it against the potential benefit, and they are willing to accept failure, whether it is launching a firm that fails or experimenting with an investment plan that does not produce outstanding results.I've been thinking a lot about risk and reward in terms of when I might quit teaching. My website had barely earned anything, and I had just taken this enormous step by quitting my job. Because blogging is a slow business model, I quickly realized that I needed an alternate source of money. I taught myself how to run Facebook advertisements for some local Investment.
The remarkable thing is that in about six months, I was out-earning my salary as a teacher, and I eventually parlayed my digital marketing talents into a highly successful digital marketing course and second business that I co-founded with my close buddy Bek Anderson

That's the short story, and it took a lot of hustle to make it work. However, I believe that this has helped me become wiser and more successful.

After that decision, I realized that taking a risk does not always lead to success or failure; you can also learn something new about yourself, discover a new skill, and end up where you are destined to be.

The idea is that successful people recognize that the potential for reward is far bigger.

2. **They know that money can buy happiness.**
Several years ago, while hanging out on my good friend's Ashley Morrie, I commented that money cannot buy happiness. His comment dramatically transformed my perspective on the subject. He went on to say, "Money by itself can't buy happiness, but it can buy or produce things that make you happy."

He meant that money can provide for early retirement, a lovely boat, a nice house, vacations, financial security, and so on.

Since that conversation with my friend, my income has improved considerably, and I can attest that I am happier with my life. I know my family has everything they need. We can have some fantastic holidays while I'm not worried out.
Money is not everything, but it certainly helps!

3. **They shamelessly self-promote.**
    There's nothing wrong with being humble. It's a good attribute, but if you're so humble that no one understands your full potential, you're doing yourself a disservice.One thing I've seen about successful people is that they quickly figure out what makes them so good at what they do. Either they will discuss it, or people they know will.

    If you struggle with talking about yourself, consider this: there is certainly someone out there who would benefit from learning more about what you do. Perhaps your tale will inspire someone else to take a risk, or you might provide advice to a friend. It's also a wonderful approach to expand your network of like-minded folks.

4. **They Know How to Sell**
    The reality is that if you want to generate money, you'll need to learn how to market items or develop your own skills. For example, I am bad at marketing in the "traditional" manner. Perhaps it's because I've always preferred a straightforward approach to the sort of sales-talk that comes across as misleading. However, understanding how to sell on my website was necessary. The same applied to learning how to offer my marketing services. I simply found a technique to accomplish it that I like.
    If you're not an entrepreneur, you still need to understand how to sell your expertise and demonstrate why you're a producer at your firm rather than a customer.

5. **They do not rely on luck:**There are several stories online about people earning $1 million or more per year while working only five hours per week. To the casual browser, these stories look to be phony or that the person is simply lucky.
The truth is that I know folks who have achieved financial success while working significantly less than the average person. But they got there by working more than 80 hours per week, running multiple side businesses, taking huge risks, and so on. Because most people can't understand that reality, it's easier to blame luck for someone's fortune or success.

Finding a mentor or buddy who has reached your goals is even better. This allows you to be around successful people as often as possible, listen carefully, ask questions, and learn.

In my perspective, there are numerous things that contribute to someone's "success." And we all have our own ideas about what success implies.It may be debt relief, establishing a business, making $5 million in investments, or something else different.

What I've attempted to do is carefully watch how these folks behave and then apply it to my own projects and life. I'm fairly convinced that it will help my internet business succeed (and some may say that it already has).

CHAPTER 8: CONCLUSION

Creating generational wealth through real estate requires strategic property investments, long-term planning, and leveraging compound growth. It necessitates a dedication to financial discipline, analyzing market patterns, and making sound decisions. Individuals who acquire and manage properties wisely can leave a lasting legacy for future generations while benefiting from the appreciation and income provided by real estate holdings over time.